Beauty for Ashes

Nakita T. Bell

DEDICATION

This devotional book is dedicated to my two darling angels –
Elizabeth and Rehema Muzaliwa.

"For the child of God, death is not the end but merely the
door into a higher and more exalted life of intimate contact
with Christ. Death is but the dark valley opening out into an
eternity of delight with God. It is not something to fear, but
an experience through which one passes on the path to a
more perfect life". - **Phillip Keller**

Rest in Heavenly Peace

Your Big Sis, Nakita

ACKNOWLEDGMENTS

I want to first and foremost acknowledge my Lord and Savior Jesus Christ. Through Him, all things are made possible.

To my husband, Steven Bell

To my Mother & Step Father, Jemma and William Mclaren

To my Grandmother, Ruth Clarke

To my Sister and Brother, Martha and Biko

To my cousins, Anthony Johnson and Alexa Clarke

I love you all

DAY 1
#BLESSED

Have you ever heard the saying "your blessing is just around the corner?" I'm sure many of us can identify with this phrase that is meant to encourage us to push forward in our faith. As I began my journey in seeking God, I was constantly reminded of the truth that He had great things in store for me. I looked forward to finding this infamous corner that everything seems to be around.

Of course, it was encouraging to hear that God would want to bless someone who at one point turned their back on Him. I would always get excited hearing this, but I started to feel discouraged as the years went on and I did not find that corner with a blessing around it.

I mean, what's with this word *blessing* anyway? Why does it always sound like it's such a distant unreachable thing that we will all get to one day by doing all of the "right things?" I know I can log on to my Instagram account or Facebook page and see the word #blessed captioned under pictures of tangible things. For example, a new car? #Blessed. New house? #Blessed. Promotion? #Blessed. I don't say this to discredit being fortunate enough to receive such things. Truly, we are blessed when we reap the benefits of hard work and God's undeserved gifts. But has our definition of the word *blessed* become completely synonymous with the definition of the "The American Dream?" You know - the nice home, stable job, three kids, and a dog?

We can easily fall prey to false perceptions of what it really means. The first thing I had to do was understand how the Bible described a blessing. Take a look at Mathew 5: 1-12. The last thing on my mind when I was praying for God's blessing was to "be poor in spirit, mourn, be meek, hungering and thirsting for righteousness, to be merciful, pure, a peacemaker, and persecuted".... Persecuted? Really?

I was waiting for more tangible things such as a dream career, a luxury car, wealth, and a huge house. But there is no hint of material prosperity in this text; so how in the world could being meek and poor in spirit lead to a life of abundant blessings? The beatitudes are extremely clear on one thing. God's richest blessings are God Himself.

Being blessed is above anything that we can obtain on this earth. It goes beyond temporal things and transcends into places that cannot be shaken by earthly disappointments. Our jobs, our cars, our wealth, and other material possessions can be taken away at any given moment. But the true blessings of God remain with us no matter what twists and turns life throws at us..

Take a look at the beatitudes and let's really evaluate our definition of being blessed in adjacent to what the Word of God outlines. God will give you heavenly insight on what it truly means to be #blessed.

"Blessed are the poor in spirit, for theirs is the kingdom of heaven. Blessed are those who mourn, for they will be comforted. Blessed are the meek, for they will inherit the earth. Blessed are those who hunger and thirst for righteousness, for they will be filled. Blessed are the merciful, for they will be shown mercy. Blessed are the pure in heart, for they will see God. Blessed are the peacemakers, for they will be called children of God. Blessed are those who are persecuted because of righteousness, for theirs is the kingdom of heaven. Blessed are you when people insult you, persecute you and falsely say all kinds of evil against you because of me." - Mathew 5:1-11

DAY 2
BEAUTIFULLY BROKEN

"And being in Bethany in the house of Simon the leper, as He sat at meat, there came a woman having an alabaster box of ointment of spikenard very precious; and she breaks the box, and poured *it* on His head." - Mark 14:3

Do you ever wonder why Mary didn't gently open her alabaster box, and pour the perfume on Jesus' head instead of dramatically breaking it? I imagine myself sitting in Jesus' place. I would've thought this woman had gone mad! First, she comes barging into the home of Simon unannounced, and then she wants to pour the substance from this broken box on my head? My first instinct would be to run away from this madness, but Jesus, on the other hand, took complete delight in her act.

To the average man or woman, anything broken becomes useless or gets thrown away into the garbage. If not thrown away, then broken items are often used for less honorable purposes or given away to charity. It wouldn't make sense to anyone in the room why Jesus was so moved by Mary as she broke this bottle of oil, then poured it on His head.

Mary was considered a sinful and adulterous woman at the time of this incident. In those days, these types of women weren't to be associated with, nor touched, especially by so-called religious men. When Mary heard that Jesus was at Simon's home, she came to meet Him with a very expensive jar of perfume, also known as an alabaster box.

Mary enters the home, sees Jesus and immediately breaks the jar and anoints His head with the perfume, then weeps at his feet and dries it with her hair. The scent of the perfume filled the entire room. Now, while everyone started whispering amongst each other about what type of woman she was, Jesus is moved and even praises her for her prostration.

So what can we learn from this story? The alabaster box can represent our past and current patterns, or even our adamant human nature. At times, in order for meaningful worship to rise up out of us, certain things have to be broken before God. In the same manner that the alabaster box was broken, and as a result, released a sweet fragrance in the room.

Mary wasn't concerned with others making judgments about where she was coming from, or how desperate she was for Jesus to restore her. Like Mary, we can also come before Jesus completely broken, and unashamed of who is watching, judging or degrading our act of worship. *Psalm 51:17* tells us that *"God will not despise a broken spirit and contrite heart."* He will fully embrace us at our lowest points. Those around you won't help but notice that sweet aroma of worship that comes out of you and fills the entire room.

The sacrifices of God *are* a broken spirit: a broken and a contrite heart, O God, thou wilt not despise. - Psalm 51:17

DAY 3
BLIND SPOTS

God has blessed me with great vision, but He has also taught me an important lesson about its limits. When I started to learn how to drive years ago, I was taught the concept of blind spots. This is an area where no matter how clear my vision is, or how perfectly adjusted my rear view mirrors are, there are zones of traffic that are blocked by the structure of my car, and that my mirrors have no view of.

I remember driving on the highway one day, and as I went to merge into another lane, I heard a long and loud honk. I swerved back into my lane and the person sped past me yelling something. I didn't hear what he said because his windows were up (Thank God!). But I realized that I was at fault because I had forgotten to check my blind spot, which could have resulted in a major accident. To be honest, this has happened to me on more than one occasion.

Spiritual blind spots are much similar to the blind spots we have while driving on the road. Despite how familiar we are with the Word of God, or how clear our visions or dreams are, there are zones of the heart and mind that we should consistently examine. On our journeys of faith in Christ, it is critical to look at these profound aspects of our life that can't be seen with our peripheral vision.

A few cases of spiritual blind spots could be a number of things. For example, blind spots might be un-forgiveness, entitlement, or even just an overwhelming to-do list that has made it impossible to recognize God's presence while doing daily tasks. We all have our own particular blind spots, and if not recognized and accounted for, they can become a risk and detrimental to our walks with God, and not only affect ourselves but also, the people around us.

7

What are some of your spiritual blind spots in life? Consider when was the last time you truly examined your heart for anything that has the potential to be hazardous to your journey with God, due to negligence.

Search me, O God, and know my heart; Try me and know my anxious thoughts. - Psalm 139:23

DAY 4
THE TRUE VINE

In *John 15:1-8*; Jesus was with 11 of His 12 disciples as the hour of His crucifixion approached. While speaking to them, He metaphorically identified Himself as the true vine, and that we are to be the branches attached to that vine. The word "true" can also be described as legitimate, a fact, a reality, an exact, and without variation.

Only Jesus can be the "true vine" to us as our source of everlasting life. In a vineyard, branches can only grow from the main grapevine, and that vine contains all necessary nutrients in order for the branch to produce leaves and fruits. Once disconnected from the vine, the branch becomes useless and cannot produce anything. The evidence that each branch is attached is the production of fruit. Jesus is the true vine and we are the branches, He is our life support and anchor. In *John 15:4*, He says *"Abide in Me, and I in you,"* so as we abide in Christ and He gives us life through His living water, we will bring forth the fruits of Christlikeness; the fruits of peace, love, forbearance, the preaching of the gospel, and a change in our community.

Another process of how branches produce fruit is the pruning. After harvest season, the dead or overgrown branches are cut away so that more fruit can grow. Pruning can be a painful process, but it is necessary for the purpose of growth. If we allow God to carefully prune us by being teachable, enduring His chastening, and ridding ourselves of negative influences - we will produce an abundance of fruit (John 15:2).

Here are some tips on how we can stay connected to Jesus:

Communication: Communication is the key to a strong, lasting, and committed relationship. *1 Thessalonians 5:17* instructs us to *"pray without ceasing."* Praying is not limited to taking place on our knees. We can talk to God in our cars, while working out, while cooking, or shopping.

Meditation: It's not enough to quickly read over our bibles. God wants us to truly reflect what we've read and apply it to our lives. In *Psalm 119:15-16, David says "I will meditate on Your precepts and regard Your ways. I will delight in Your statutes and not forget Your word."* It's also important for us to refrain from entertaining negative thoughts. *Philippians 4:8* says, *"Whatever is true, honorable, right, pure, lovely, and of good repute, meditate on these things."*

Surroundings: I realized a major difference in my life when I surrounded myself with like-minded people. I couldn't get to where I needed to be in my personal journey by keeping company with just anyone. I don't mean to suggest that we ought to shun others or place ourselves on a pedestal. But the bible says in *1 Corinthians 15:33*, that *"evil company corrupts good habits."* Thus, our company can make or break us.

Motives: Everything mentioned above becomes useless if our motives aren't right. Imagine having a friend that clings to you only because of what you have to offer. I guarantee you that they won't be around for long. God sees and knows our hearts. Look at *James 4:3*, God will not answer certain prayers, simply because they are being asked with the wrong motives. *Mathew 6:1* also talks about practicing our righteousness with a motive to be seen by people. Jesus says, *"for such things there is no reward,"* …yikes! See Galatians 1:10 as well, are we seeking the approval of people? Or God? Motives are POWERFUL. Let's reflect on the reasons why we want to be connected to Jesus.

Jesus is our true source of strength. The key to fruitfulness and life more abundantly is our connection to Him, the true vine. In Him we will prevail and in Him we always win. *John 15:7* tells us that if we abide in Him, and His Word is in us, we can ask whatever we will and it will be done for us. What a promise!

Abide in Me, and I in you. As the branch cannot bear fruit of itself unless it abides in the vine so neither can you unless you abide in Me. I am the vine and you are the branches. He who abides in Me and I in him, he bears much fruit; for apart from Me, you can do nothing. – John 15:4-5

DAY 5
DESIGNED FOR DOMINION

At the very beginning of creation, God gave us an unfathomable responsibility to rule over all that He created here on earth. Not just specific regions, but over all of the earth as indicated in *Gen 1:26*. Can you imagine? The Creator of the universe gave us the privilege of managing the work of His hands! There was no interview process to see who was qualified for the position of management, and there was no "working your way to the top". Rather, He gave us this task automatically and for an unspecified amount of time, Adam and Eve got to enjoy this privilege consecutively.

While in the Garden of Eden, Satan came along in the form of a snake and tricked Eve into eating a fruit from a tree that God gave instructions forbidding them to eat from. Due to disobedience, when Adam followed his wife and ate the fruit, we lost the dominion that was originally given over the earth to us. This would mean that we are now hopeless and subject to the limitations of this world and that we can no longer exercise dominion. This would mean that Satan now has control over the earth and that our relationship with God is completely severed and damaged.

This is the narrative Satan still wants us to believe. While this may have been true at one point in history, it was reversed when Jesus died on the cross and restored us to God's original plan. He restored everything to us that Adam lost in the Garden of Eden.

So, how do we exercise dominion again now that it's been restored through Christ? It's helpful to think of it this way: God's original plan was for us to be caretakers of the earth, and also His representatives. Now, I'm no environmentalist, but it's obvious that we are not living in complete paradise when we consider our current trends in pollution, animal extinction, demolished forests and climate change. Of course, exercising dominion is way more than just recycling, and using environment-friendly products. It's about being representatives of Christ through our *character and habits*, and acting as God would towards everything here on earth.

It's not always easy to live as redeemed people in a fallen world. But let's work towards being ambassadors for Christ by using every opportunity possible to glorify Him. We are a chosen people, designed to show the world what God is like.

Then God said, "Let us make man in our image, after our likeness. And let them have dominion over the fish of the sea and over the birds of the heavens and over the livestock and over all the earth and over every creeping thing that creeps on the earth." - Genesis 1:26

DAY 6
DOES GOD STILL SPEAK?

Does it ever seem like God speaks and addresses everyone but you? Do you ever feel like your supplications aren't going anywhere other than hitting the roof of your room, or that you're simply conversing with thin air? Years ago, I used to be extremely skeptical of others claiming to have "heard from the Lord". To be honest, I would flat-out roll my eyes. In my mind, I would think, what do you mean that you heard from God? Was speaking to God just like having a regular conversation with my companions, in which you could literally hear each other's voices? Is it trailed by a split of thunder and lightning? What do you mean by "God told me?" I was numb to those statements because I didn't take anyone seriously when they said anything remotely near hearing "Gods voice". I knew God existed, yet I got to a place where I needed to move past the theology and really hear Him for myself.

God speaking is probably one of the most misunderstood truths in the faith as we automatically associate it with ONLY an audible voice or our understanding of communication. It can cause sentiments of perplexity, rejection, and may make you feel inferior believing that God never addresses you. In all actuality, God is consistently speaking and speaks in different ways. The real question is; are we tuned in? Are we listening? We live in a world that is getting noisier by the day. Whether the hassles of our careers, governmental issues, kids, deferred housework, and social media networking, trying to recognize God's voice can be frustrating, but it is certainly not impossible.

It truly involves blocking out the commotion of the world and taking time during our devotional portion of the day to wait on Him in silence. We get so used to doing all of the talking during our prayer time, and sometimes never give God the chance to speak. Imagine speaking to a friend on the telephone, and you do the majority of the talking and then say "alright bye" once you're finished, not giving them a chance to speak or respond to the things you've said. That is discourteous if you ask me. Yet, this is often our reality with God - we do all the talking, then say "alright, amen" and hop into bed, not giving Him a chance to speak.

God does speak audibly when He wants to, but it's about permitting the Holy Spirit to address your heart which also comes by ruminating over His word. In *1 Kings 19:12*, the Prophet Elijah depicts it as a *"still small voice,"* so no wonder it can easily be muffled by the noisy matters of our regular daily existence. It won't come overnight, but learning to sit in stillness, with an expectant heart, and meditating on His word will allow for you to hear God clearly. We are His sheep, and God's desire is to have a two-way communication with us.

My sheep hear my voice, and I know them, and they follow Me. – John 10:27

DAY 7
ATTITUDE CHECK

Challenges arise from every aspect of life as a maturing human being. We all have our moments when our attitudes are not so pleasant, nor welcoming to others. There are so many things that can alter our attitudes including, a sudden change of plans, a change in the weather, a change in our health, or sometimes the actions of others.

For the most part, our outward attitudes and responses reflect and display what's truly going on in our hearts. If you're filled with joy on the inside, it will show externally; if you're filled with negativity, that too will also be evident. It's inevitable that we will encounter tragedies and challenges in our lifetime, but our outlook and how we approach them will determine our success in overcoming them.

While may not have been born with positive attitudes, it is something we can choose to develop over time. In the book *Attitude 101 written by John Maxwell* – He mentions that 87.5% of our success is based on our attitudes, while the remaining 12.5% is based on our knowledge (or skills). Despite how skilled we are in building, fixing and business - or how knowledgeable we may be, our perception of life and the conditions of our hearts can make or break the success of these attributes.

In *Philippians 2:14-15*, the Apostle Paul tells us to *"do all things without complaining, and grumbling"*. We are the light in a hopeless world and letting our lights shine directly affects our attitudes. It would be easy to tell someone to put on a Christ-like attitude, but what does that actually look like?

Let's look at a couple of examples from the bible:

Love – "Therefore, be imitators of God as dearly loved children and *live in love*, just as Christ also loved us and gave himself for us, a sacrificial and fragrant offering to God". - Ephesians 5:1 & 2

Forgive – "Bearing with one another and forgiving one another, if someone happens to have a complaint against anyone else. Just as the Lord has *forgiven you*, so you also *forgive others*". – Colossians 3:13

Be Kind – "But love your enemies, and do good, and lend, expecting nothing back. Then your reward will be great, and you will be sons of the Most High, because *He is kind to* ungrateful and evil people". – Luke 6:35

According to Mathew 15:18; it is "what comes out of us that defiles us". Reflect on your recent attitude towards a situation, a family member, a friend, or even your spouse. Consider the vertical aspect of those attitudes. Did it reflect or demonstrate God's character? As mentioned, we are the light in a dark and hopeless world, and letting our lights shine has an inseparable tie with our attitudes.

Will you accept the challenge of working towards being kind, forgiving, and loving consistently? I know I'm still working on it.

Do all things without grumbling or questioning, that you may be blameless and innocent, children of God without blemish in the midst of a crooked and twisted generation, among whom you shine as lights in the world. - Philippians 2:14-15

DAY 8
MY SPIRITUAL WINTER

There was a very wise man in the Bible by the name of Solomon. He stated these six very profound words; "To everything there is a season" - Ecclesiastes 3:1-2, meaning that there is an appropriate time for everything.

As I was reading about winter on the Internet, it became even more evident why I dislike the season so much. Winter is extremely dormant and cold. The days become shorter, there isn't as much sun, you get frost bites, flowers die, trees become bare, and there is no sign of the green pastures or still waters that God talks about. Instead, what do I see? I see frozen water, dirty slush, and a field of ice and snow banks.

I often asked myself "why did God even create winter?" Especially on days when I was almost late for work. You know, those days when you don't wait for your car to fully warm up, so you drive with a semi-frozen windshield and can barely see? Then you try to spray windshield fluid thinking it will help, only for it to freeze over? On top of that, you're shivering while driving - If you know me, you know that I just do not get along with cold weather.

A spiritually dormant season is much like winter. You're praying, you're fasting, you're studying the word, and still, you're stuck in a season of barrenness and darkness, where nothing seems to grow. It's hard to believe that this particular time in your life is all a part of God's plan. Winter is a season designed by God, for a specific time. It is not meant to ruin our lives, but instead, we can use this season as a time to start planning and preparing for the coming seasons.

While we cannot parallel our spiritual seasons with the four major natural seasons, we understand that there is a very key similarity; they are both always changing. Although you may feel like God isn't with you in your spiritual winter, He is. I am still learning how to embrace my natural winter. Whenever I complain about the cold weather, my husband always says the same thing to me, "learn to love it!" I am squirming on the inside every time he says it, but he makes a good point. It may even help to go outside and catch a snowflake on my tongue (which won't happen), go skating, sledding, or take photos of the beautiful ice dams on windows.

As hard as it is for me to admit it, there are many benefits throughout the winter. Here are a few of them that I found on *mamiverse.com*.

1. It's better for sleeping.
2. It increases your energy.
3. It produces cleaner air for better breathing.
4. My absolute favorite- NO BUGS!

Be encouraged and embrace the season that you are in. Know that all things are working for your good. The bible states that "no discipline brings joy, but seems grievous and painful, but afterwards it yields a peaceable fruit of righteousness to those who have been trained by it". – Hebrews 12:11

To everything there is a season, and a time to every purpose under the heaven. A time to be born, and a time to die. A time to plant, and a time to pluck up that which is planted. A time to kill, and a time to heal. A time to break down, and a time to build up. A time to weep, and a time to laugh. A time to mourn, and a time to dance. A time to cast away stones, and a time to gather stones together. A time to embrace, and a time to refrain from embracing. A time to get, and a time to lose. A time to keep, and a time to cast away. A time to rend, and a time to sew. A time to keep silent, and a time to speak. A time to love, and a time to hate. A time of war, and a time of peace. – Ecclesiastes 3:1

DAY 9
A FATHER'S LOVE

For many of us, when we hear the term father, it can release all kinds of different emotions, both negative and positive. For some, it may release a sense of rejection and abandonment, while for others it may be comfort, security, and protection. Each one of us *may* have been let down by our earthly father in one way or another; whether it was by minor mistakes that we got over the next day, or huge disappointments that left scars and wounds. We can see throughout scripture that fatherhood, whether spiritual or biological, is a position ordained by God.

When we accept Christ as our Savior, He becomes our Heavenly Father, and we become His daughters. Sometimes, it may be extremely hard to embrace the Fatherly aspect of God because our view may have been a little distorted due to our relationships with our earthly fathers. But guess what? God's love for you is so big, and He proved it by giving His life as a ransom for you. See John 3:16.

It's breathtaking to know that the King of all Kings in His holy dwelling; chose to describe Himself as a Father to us. Consider how a little child clings to their father and mother and becomes reliant on their parents for everything. This is how God wants us to rely on Him, with complete trust and dependency. He invites us in Mark 10:13-16, to come to Him as little children.

You can turn to God when you need approval, attention, and comfort. You can cry out "Abba, Father" and He will answer. He is a consistent and competent Father, and will never leave you or forsake you.

But when the right time came, God sent His Son, born of a woman, subject to the law. God sent Him to but freedom for us who were slaves to the law, so that He could adopt us as His very own children, and because we are His children, God has sent us the spirit of His Son into our hearts, prompting us to cry out, "Abba, Father." – Galations 4:4-6

DAY 10
THE DANGER OF SELF-PITY

When we feel pity towards someone, we are expressing a form of compassion and empathy, and may feel an unction to do something to help. We can feel this exact same emotion towards ourselves, referred to as self-pity. It is completely healthy to express that we have been hurt, or acknowledge that something didn't go as planned. But the problem with self-pity begins when we allow situations to persist, and instead of feeling compelled to help ourselves, we end up in a place of helplessness or victimhood.

Self-pity can be very subtle and become heart-hardening. It encourages us to find comfort in our place of misery while waiting for justice to be served – even if all that happened was a situation didn't go our way. This doesn't take away the fact that we have suffered injustice, but the truth is, we have the duty to forgive regardless of whether or not we receive an apology. God is not insensitive to what bothers us. But He doesn't want us to unpack and live in our offences.

See Luke chapter 22, as Jesus was nailed to the cross; He didn't cry out "Father, punish them for what they are doing," Nor did He yell "All of you owe me an apology". Instead, He said, "Father, forgive them, for they know not what they do". Jesus is the reason that we are forgiven, and also the reason we can forgive others. As children of God, we have not been given a spirit of offence, grief, or helplessness; this is contrary to what the word says. In 2 Corinthians 3:17, it states that "where The Spirit of The Lord is, there is liberty" which means we have the ability to live in freedom…not self-pity.

Letting go of hurt and pain can be a hard thing to do, especially when wrongdoings are lodged into our unfading memories. But letting go is simpler than we think. We let go by giving up what is beyond our control. We can't undo what has been done in the past, and we can't control hurtful words that shaped the state of our hearts. But what we can do is allow the truth of the scriptures to reshape our hearts, and hold on to the new things that God has promised us. Isaiah 43:18-19 says, "Do not remember the former things, nor consider the things of old, 'Behold, I will do a new thing".

How can we see the new that God wants to do in our lives if we are constantly holding on to old emotions? I can assure you that you do not want to miss out on God's promises. Let's give up on looking back, and let it go once and for all. Releasing yourself will not only benefit you, but it will also benefit the generations coming after you.

Then Peter came up and said to Him, "Lord, how often should I forgive someone who sins against me? As many as seven times?" Jesus said to him, "not seven times, but seventy times seven." – Mathew 18: 21-22

DAY 11
LOYALTY

Between 1495 and 1498, Leonardo da Vinci painted a fascinating depiction of Jesus and His 12 disciples breaking bread at the Last Supper. This painting is hung up in our dining rooms, kitchens, dining halls, and this historical moment is also observed in our church sanctuaries. I have to confess, there was a time where I would partake in communion, and not truly dismiss the distractions in my life, and instead, gave my divided attention to Jesus. Sure, I would close my eyes and reflect on what communion represents, but then once I swallowed those crackers and drank the grape juice; it was back to business as usual.

I can only imagine what the disciples were feeling at the Lord's Supper. I can imagine hearts racing, troubled spirits, and the confusion of not fully understanding what Jesus was saying. For them, Jesus was a friend they had been following for the last three years, and now He was telling them that He was about to leave. Not only did He forewarn them that His time had come, but He also revealed upcoming denial and betrayal. Peter, who Jesus loved, was forewarned that he would deny Him, not once, but three times. We can be quick to condemn Peter, but has there ever been a time where we've also betrayed Jesus? I will admit that there have been moments I've remained silent when I should have spoken up for Him, and there have also been moments where I've been too timid to admit that I have a personal relationship with Him. What about Judas? Could we admit that we have turned our backs on God at one point or another and completely betrayed Him?

Jesus loves each and every one of us, and it's evident in the fact that He spent His last supper with men who He knew would betray and deny Him. He knew what He had to face but still remained loyal to His Father's will.

Self-examination is one of the most crucial practices in obtaining a healthy spiritual life and journey with God. It may help us to examine our level of loyalty to Him every now and again. While we are still human, and our loyalty may fail at times, Gods loyalty towards us never will.

Then he called the crowd to him along with his disciples and said: "Whoever wants to be my disciple must deny themselves and take up their cross and follow me. – Mathew 16-24

DAY 12
FINDING PEACE WITHIN THE CHAOS

By nature, women can be some of the world's biggest multi-taskers. We can clean the house while talking on the phone; we can do assignments for school/work while planning our dinner for the week, or fold laundry while reorganizing our cupboards at the same time. Regardless of this superpower, we still succumb to the feeling of being overwhelmed every now and again.

Whether it is related to school, kids, work, bills, or a project we are working on, we profoundly realize our human limitations and capacities once things are out of our control. Often times we don't even understand how we got to this point. It could be a series of bad choices, taking on too many tasks, juggling too many things at once, being overall disorganized, or life just simply throwing its curve balls.

When we are in those moments of feeling maxed out and wanting to crash or give up on everything. We may ask ourselves this one simple question: who put me here? Did God bring me to this point of borderline explosion? God will stretch you and test you, but He will never give you so many tasks to the point where things become out of control. It's not His desire for us to feel bombarded and overthrown. In those moments of struggling to stay afloat, or feeling like a hamster on a wheel, realize that you are only one person and you sometimes need to just stop and be still. Be still in your heart, mind, and soul.

Feeling bombarded can easily make you vulnerable to giving up, but in those moments you can also allow God to help you regain perspective and look to Him for help. Jesus said that His yoke is easy and His burden is light. It's okay for you to tell Him that you feel you are juggling more than you can handle, and it's okay to tell Him that you are burnt out. This is what He wants you to do. You are not lazy for wanting a break from it all, nor are you neglecting your responsibilities. In moments like this, He promises to give us rest.

Then Jesus said, "come to Me, all of you who are weary and carry heavy burdens, and I will give you rest. Take My yoke upon you. Let Me teach you, because I am humble and gentle at heart, and you will find rest for your souls. For My yoke is easy to bear, and the burden I give you is light." – Mathew 11:28-30

DAY 13
IN HIS IMAGE AND LIKENESS

In Genesis 1:1 – We observe that the universe and everything in it was created by God. Just by this one verse, we can see how great God really is. He divided the day from the night, separated light from darkness, created the grass and the herbs yielding seed after its kind, and saw that this was all good. Just like the elements mentioned, we were also created by God. When God created the animals, vegetation, and all the herbs, He created them after their kind, and they were only able to produce after their kind. Man, on the other hand, was created after the "God-kind" in His very own image and likeness.

When we hear the term "image and likeness," we may automatically assume that the bible is strictly talking about a more physical manifestation of God such as our fingers, eyes, ears, and the rest of our bodily form. But there is a more intellectual, social, and moral likeness that we mirror. We exhibit attributes that God Himself embodies.

To name a few:

Our ability to create: Isaiah 64:8 – Oh Lord, You are our Father; we are the clay, and You are the potter; we are all the work of Your hand.

Our ability to love: 1 john 3:1 – See what kind of love the Father has given to us, that we should be called children of God; and so we are.

Our ability to see: Job 34:21 – For God watches how people live; He sees everything they do.

Our ability to hear: 1 John 5:14 – And this is the confidence that we have toward Him, that if we ask anything according to His will, He hears us.

Our ability to breathe: Genesis 2:7 – Then the Lord God formed the man from the dust of the ground. He breathed the breath of life into the man's nostrils.

Our ability to move: Genesis 1:2 – The earth was formless and void, and darkness was over the surface of the deep, and the Spirit of God was moving over the surface of the waters.

We are spiritual beings: John 4:24 – God is Spirit, and His worshippers must worship Him in Spirit and in truth.

These attributes were given to us so that we can have a true relationship with God to a degree that is even greater than His angels. When we fully embrace our likeness to God, we will realize our untapped potential. Although He created us all in His image, He is imprinted differently and uniquely in every single person. Therefore, there is only one you and you are special.

So God created mankind in His own image, in the image of God He created him; male and female He created them. - Genesis 1:27

DAY 14
ENVY MAKES THE BONES ROT

Cases and consequences of envious hearts can be found all over the bible. One of the first cases here on earth was between Cain and Abel, the first recorded sons of Adam and Eve. Cain slew Abel because he was envious of his brothers offering to God; Abel brought exactly what God had required, while on the other hand, Cain brought the opposite. This resulted in Abel committing the first murder in humanity, all in the name of envy.

Feelings of envy arise when we feel entitled to something that someone else has. Envy has sadly been a driving force behind a lot of severed friendships and relationships. It may even get to the point where we find more comfort in another individual's failures rather than an achievement, and giving a genuine compliment becomes very difficult.

This is not the heart of God, and envy shows that we are not operating in His wisdom or character. James 3:14-15 says, *"but if you have bitter jealousy and selfish ambition in your hearts, do not boast and be false to the truth. This is not the wisdom that comes down from above, but is earthly, unspiritual, and demonic"*.

A heart filled with envy, is often a heart that is filled with discontent. God wants us to be content and grateful for what we have because ultimately, it's what He has given us. I was taught that anytime I feel emotions that I know aren't coming from God, to refer to *2 Corinthians 10:5* and say this out loud and over myself *"I cast down all imaginations, and every high thing that exalts itself against the knowledge of God, and bringing into captivity every thought to make it obedient to Christ."*

We have the power to not just *slay* our eyebrows, shoes, and outfits. We have the power to slay principalities and rulers of darkness in our lives, including envy. We have the power to decide that certain things just cannot stay.

Below are two helpful thoughts to consider if you ever feel emotions of envy:

Avoid comparing yourself to others – The more we count the blessings of others, the more we will miss out on our own.

Recognize your uniqueness – God has designed a custom-made life for you. This includes all of your unique gifts and talents. Begin to make a list of the things you're good at and write down what you like about yourself. This is not boasting in yourself, but rather, identifying the traits that make you unique. You will certainly find that you compare yourself less and less to others. The competition will become irrelevant because you know you have your own calling and purpose to fulfill.

A peaceful heart gives life to the body, but envy makes the bones rot. - Proverbs 14:30

DAY 15
ON THE DEFENSE

Our responses to situations, and how we react towards others when confronted, depend on many different factors. For example; you may have a short fuse or could be quick-tempered because of past relationships, being bullied at a specific stage in your life, abuse, or even low self-esteem could play a part in being extremely vulnerable when being approached.

Pola Muzyka, the Author of - Free from the stronghold of defensiveness, stated that *"A person with a defensive spirit is excessively concerned with guarding against the real or imagined threat of criticism, injury to one's ego, or exposure of one's shortcomings. The host puts up walls and may see an offense where none is intended."*

To put it in simple terms, a defensive person is obsessed with protecting themselves against legitimate or illegitimate threats. We can ask ourselves these questions to know whether or not we are struggling with defensiveness:

1. Do I always feel that people are wishing ill, or thinking negative thoughts towards me?
2. Do I get offended when receiving *constructive criticism*
3. Do I always feel the need to justify, legitimize, or make excuses for actions, rather than embracing change and/or corrections?
4. Do I shut people out and give myself a list of reasons why?
5. Am I constantly in a "fight or flight" frame of mind? This is a mode where your brain senses threatening

situations, and you are forced with the decision to run or fight back.

Defeating defensiveness is important because it forms walls built from our own strength, which ends up substituting God's protection. How do we silence that inner-lawyers constant scream to defend ourselves? How do we stop this stronghold from destroying our relationships and invite animosity and paranoia? Ridding ourselves of defensive tendencies will start by identifying the root of the trait. God may even begin to show you things from your childhood. It may sound senseless and irrelevant, but it's important to understand that the *some* of the issues in our adult life; are an immediate reflection of what has happened in our childhood life.

Having a Christ-like attitude does not rely on upon how you are dealt with and treated by others, but it is the means by which you react. God wants his daughters to be forgiving, teachable, and receptive to correction. I've learned (the hard way) that correction is an amazing thing although it's an extremely hard pill to swallow at times. It helps me stay on course and helps me grow in wisdom. *Proverbs 8:11* says that *"Wisdom is better than jewels, and all that you may desire cannot compare with her"*. Personally, I want to be a wise woman and not a silly one.

But the fruit of the Spirit is love, joy, peace, forbearance, kindness, goodness, faithfulness, gentleness and self-control. Against such things there is no law. – Galations: 5-22-23

DAY 16
AN ORDINARY DAY WITH EXTRAORDINARY PURPOSE

Life can appear to be so monotonous and predictable to a considerable amount of us. From the minute we open up our eyes we know precisely how our day will start and end. Wake up, shower, have breakfast, run out the door, go to work or school for a large portion of the day, get back home, eat dinner, clean up, read a chapter or two of the Bible, say a prayer, go to sleep, and the next day do it all again....You know, the usual. This may make us feel so insignificant for the duration of the day on the grounds that, having an ordinary day as a Christian is contradictory, right?

Within our walks with God, we *sometimes* develop a notion that being a Christian means that our name has one day got to someday make it in the limelight. Whether it is plastered everywhere on social media or broadcasted on television to make our life count. While becoming internationally known may happen and is *not wrong*, it still shouldn't be at the front line of our thoughts when it comes to carrying on with an existence that pleases God.

The psalmist said that *"this is the day that The Lord has made, we will rejoice and be glad in it."* No matter what boring routine we may feel that we're circling in; this is a day that God created, and we should rejoice knowing that He's allowed us to be a part of it.

God is always working on what seems to be an ordinary day and uses ordinary people to carry out His extraordinary plan. There's a story recorded in *Judges 6* about a man named Gideon who was called by God to deliver Israel from an evil group named the Midianites. They were so cruel to the point that the Israelites had to hide in mountains and caves from them

34

(Judges 6:2). On an ordinary day, doing his regular duties - Gideon was threshing wheat at the bottom of a winepress, when an angel appeared to him. Can you imagine being at work on what appears to be a regular day, and then suddenly you're standing in front of an angel?

The angel then tells Gideon to "go with the strength you have, and rescue Israel from the Midianites. I am sending you." Gideon replies by telling the angel that he is the least in his family and that his clan is the weakest in his tribe (Judges 6:14-15). What Gideon was failing to understand at this moment, was that it wasn't about what he was, or wasn't capable of. The Lord said to him *"I will be with you, and you will destroy the Midianites as if you were fighting against one man."* This had nothing to do with what Gideon was capable of or what his day consisted of. God wanted to use Gideon to do His work by assuring him that He was with him.

Gideon's obedience brought victory to Israel, and God used three hundred men to win the battle against the Midianites. Today, He is still a God who uses ordinary people, on an ordinary day, to carry out an extraordinary plan. We can become liberated to God's purpose, once we realize that the only thing extraordinary about us is the God that lives in us.

This is the day the LORD has made. We will rejoice and be glad in it. - Psalm 118:24

DAY 17
DIAMONDS ARE A GIRLS BEST FRIEND

Most woman are unquestionably fascinated by diamonds. In my opinion, no other gemstone is as beautiful, mesmerizing, or as stunning as the diamond. For centuries, this stone has been described as a symbol for eternal love. It is the number one choice when it comes to engagement rings, anniversary and, Valentine's Day gifts, and men are actually encouraged to spend two-three months of their salary on this precious stone for their significant other.

Most of us have heard the term "diamonds are forever" by De Beer's Diamond Jewelry, and the basic description of this slogan is that a diamond is supposed to represent eternal love, and also refers to them being hardest substance known to mankind. The process of a diamond is what makes it even more unique and everlasting, but what some of us don't know, is that the diamond is a by-product of a *not so mesmerizing* process. Here are a few of the phases we don't see when it comes to diamonds:

Pressurization – Long before we see diamonds beautifully and neatly displayed in our favorite jewelry stores, they are underneath the ground we walk on and formed under extreme temperature and pressure. You can imagine that it's dark, cold, hidden, secluded, and lonely down there. The pressure of the whole world is on your back, literally.

Eruption – Under the high pressure, atoms bond together forming crystals, they lock into place and eventually grow large enough to produce visible crystals. These crystals then rise to the surface of the earth through a volcanic activity which is imaginably violent. Once brought to the surface; the volcanic material eventually cools, and diamonds are contained within this material.

Cutting – Once retrieved, diamonds undergo sorting and sawing, carefully studied, cut and polished in its own unique way.

I can tell you by experience, that pressure and being in what seems to be a cold and dark place is never fun, and probably not what you'd wish your life would be at any point. The wonderful thing about God is that He has given us so many visible and tangible manifestations of what His desire and plan is for our lives. He wants to take us out of a state of pressure and loneliness, and make us into something beautiful and unique. Each one of us has been handpicked by God and uniquely cut, displaying the work of our heavenly Father's Hands.

But he knows where I am going, and when he tests me, I will come out as *gold*. - Job 23:10

DAY 18
REMEMBER YOUR CREATOR

In *Ecclesiastes 12:1* – Solomon encourages us to remember God while we are still young. Our enemy tries to convince us that our youth is for our own pleasures, and tampering with the temptations of the world. I mean, we should be able to party and experiment with drugs while we're young right? They say "you only live once" and the time to have fun is now. Maybe I'll consider serving God and being religious when I'm old.

Why is it that we are encouraged to remember God in our youth? Why now? Why not when we've settled down and experienced everything that this world has to offer? My question is this – why wait until we're older and running low on energy to fully serve our Creator?

Here are a few reasons why it's best to remember God now:

Our motivation in life is at its highest when we are young.
In *Ecclesiastes 12:1* Solomon writes that *"the years are coming when you will say, I have no pleasure in them."* Basically meaning that there will come a day when you have no pleasure, or ambition in life anymore. You just want to relax. Why not dedicate our ambitions in life while we're young, to the One who created us?
Physically, you're more energetic when you're young.
I believe God deserves us when we are most energetic and can perform to the best of our abilities. He deserves our best years. *Ecclesiastes 12:3-5* reminds us that there will come a time when our body starts to change and we won't have the strength we once did when we were young. (Serving God in our older years

is by no means less meaningful than serving Him in our younger years)

Peer pressure is at its highest when we are young.
It can be a lot more challenging to think about God when we are young. We're dealing with hormones, pressures of marriage, kids, career paths, and immortality. This is why we need our Creator now more than ever, to help us through this battlefield of life and all of our decisions.

Remembering God is more than just thinking about Him once in a blue moon. It's about allowing Him to guide us in every decision we make. God's desire is that we live a life that pleases Him, but also that we enjoy life for ourselves. Some experiences are necessary, but there are some mistakes that can be avoided if we always remember Him and include Him in our walks of life.

Remember now the Creator in the days of your youth, while evil days have not come, or the years draw nigh when you will says "I have no pleasure in them" – Ecclesiastes 12:1

DAY 19
YOU ARE CHOSEN!

When we think of a heroine, we often associate it with specific character traits such as strong, savvy, a streak of rebellion, adventurous, impulsive, nerdy by day, exotic by night, and that alpha female kind of attitude. The last thing we would ever think of, is that a poor orphaned girl living in captivity could one day become the heroine of an entire Nation.

Esther was a motherless and fatherless young Jewish girl being raised by her cousin Mordecai, during the captivity of the Jews in Persia. When King Ahasuerus, (the king of Persia) put on a banquet for his nobles and officials, he got drunk and then called for his wife - Queen Vashti, to show her off to everyone. When she refused to come, King Ahasuerus became furious and banishes her from the kingdom, calling on a nation-wide pageant for a new Queen

Little did Esther know she would be rounded up out of the blue with all of the other maidens so that he could choose his new wife. These women had to go through special beauty regimes and purging before being presented to the king. Esther, as we know, was chosen and found the most attractive out of all of the women. During this time, one of the king's officials by the name of Haman; (the Adolph Hitler of the Old Testament) had a plan to massacre all of the Jews that were living in Persia.

Now, can you imagine being held captive in a country, and then you're randomly chosen to be an option for a wife to an evil king? To top it off, this is the King who would eventually issue a decree to kill your people. The last thing I would be thinking is that God had some sort of plan throughout all of this. We're talking about a poor, orphaned girl who is now about to become the wife of a drunkard of a king; has to hide her Jewish identity, and yet God has a plan for all of this?

At that time, by law, you were not allowed to approach the king without being asked. Mordecai overhears of a plan to have the king assassinated and quickly informs Esther. Mordecai prompts Esther to intervene and convinces her that she was most likely chosen for the deliverance of her people… "if you remain completely silent at this time, relief and deliverance will arise for the Jews from another place, but you and your father's house will perish. Yet who knows whether you have come to the kingdom for such a time as this?"- Esther 4:14. Basically, he was telling her that there was no mistake in her being where she was, at that particular time.

Mordecai understood what was at stake, and Esther decided to risk her life by approaching the king. She made a very bold statement - "If I perish, I perish," but she was going to plead with the king if it was the last thing she did. Here, we have a courageous and bold queen in the right place at the right time, who didn't care what could happen to her. What I love the most about Esther is she didn't sit around throwing a tantrum about what she was about to face. It says in *Esther 4:16* that she gathered her maidens and asked them to fast for her. *Sometimes* as women, our first instinct is to react in an emotional manner. We don't know for certain what Esther was feeling at this particular time, but we know from what was recorded, that she handled her business by going to the Lord.

Imagine if we tried Esther's approach and instead fought on our knees as our first option? He fasting and prayer brought clarity and deliverance. Esther also didn't approach the king with an attitude, but the bible says she put on her best apparel, got all dazzled up, waited for the king, and then approached him humbly. No wonder she was offered up to half of his kingdom.

Eventually, the plan to set the Jews free was accomplished and this decree was sealed and irreversible - *Esther 8:8*. God used this woman who was literally a nobody at the time, for such an amazing moment in history. We all have a *"for such a time as this"* moment and our assignment is just as important. Lives are at stake, and we are surrounded by people daily who God desperately wants to rescue. We can step out boldly just as Esther did for such a time as this. You have an amazing purpose and have been called out by name to bring the gospel of hope to a lost world.

Be strong and courageous. Do not be afraid or terrified because of them, for the Lord God goes with you, He will never leave you or forsake you. – Deuteronomy 31:6

DAY 20
BE CAREFUL LITTLE TONGUE WHAT YOU SAY

We've all heard the saying "you are what you eat," meaning if you eat healthily, you are healthy, and if you eat unhealthy, you are unhealthy. I'm a firm believer that it is the exact same concept when it comes to the words we speak. If you speak negative things, you will begin you live a negative life, and if you speak positive things, you will begin to have a more positive outlook on life. It is as simple as that. Your words shape your ideas, your concepts, perspectives, and they also form your habits.

Speaking life and positivity doesn't mean that you're being ignorant to a difficult situation, or that you're naive. It means that you understand that by your words and by faith, you have the power to change a situation, and you're trusting God to work things out for your good.

In James 3, he describes the tongue as such a small member of the body, but just as all it takes is a little match to start a forest fire, so can the tongue defile the whole body. God makes it very clear in His word how *powerful* our words are and how they shape our world. He reveals to us in Proverbs 18:21 that "the power of life and death lies in the tongue!" It was by words that this world was made, and words are also what God chose to communicate with us, and to us.

It's important to understand the seriousness of what we allow to come out of our mouths. When we're addressing each other, let's be mindful of the fact that once we speak hurtful words, we cannot just automatically take it back. Words can be harmful, or they can be used to be a blessing, but not both. James 3:10 says "Out of the same mouth comes blessings and cursing's, my sisters and brothers, these things should not be so." James is saying we cannot speak both blessings and curses from the same mouth.

We can be a lot more cautious with what we say by being slow to speak. I've learned that there's nothing wrong with having delayed responses. It may help to think of these questions before speaking:

- Is what I'm about to say necessary?
- Will what I'm about to say edify?
- What are my intentions in what I'm about to say?
- Will what I'm about to say, upset God?

It may seem like a lot to think of before speaking. But when we understand the power of our words, we realize that it can be a tool used to change the world around us for the greater good, but can also destroy it.

Let no corrupting talk come out of your mouths, but only such as is good for building up, as fits the occasion, that it may give grace to those who hear. – Ephesians 4:29

DAY 21
THIRSTY

In John 4:1-9, Jesus and His disciples were on their way to Galilee and had to travel through a town called Samaria. The disciples went to look for food, and Jesus being tired and weary sat down by a well. He meets a Samaritan woman there and asks her to provide water for Him to drink. The woman immediately responds by telling Him that Jews and Samaritans have nothing to do with each other and weren't even supposed to speak.

Jesus responds by telling her that *"if she were to only realize the gift of God standing before her, she would have asked Him for a drink, and He would have given her living water"* - John 4:10. The woman, missing the spiritual meaning behind what He said, now asks Jesus where His bucket was, and where He will get this living water. Logically, her question was valid - you need a bucket to draw water from a well. But the water Jesus was talking about wasn't literal water to quench your thirst. Instead, it was spiritual water that would satisfy this woman so deeply she would never thirst again. The woman then takes Him up on His offer for this living water (John 4:15).

Jesus began to reveal things about her life that only she would know. Things that proved she was in need of more than a physical quenching, and in her specific case - it was her multiple husbands. Have you ever ran back to the same old issues expecting different results, or a different turnout? Whether it was a specific relationship, a career path, certain types of friends, attention, or anything that makes you feel good temporarily but leaves you unsatisfied?

Jesus gently exposes her issue, and she starts to question whether He was the Messiah or not. I mean, how else would He know all that He did? At this point after realizing who He was, the woman runs back to her village telling every one of her encounter with Him.

Many people in today's society are suffering from spiritual thirst. We don't even realize it's spiritual, so we turn to physical solutions hoping to quench a spiritual dehydration. We all possess a type of void in our lives in one way or another. But have we ever stopped to ask ourselves why we keep running back to the same solutions? Especially when Jesus made an eternal promise that we would never be thirsty after drinking from His water.

The same Jesus who visited the Samaritan woman at the well is the same Jesus that lives today and His redeeming offer still stands. We don't have to settle for temporary solutions, when He has offered us living water. This is not literal water you can get from your tap or a river. What He was referring to was the gift of eternal life (John 4:14).

We can continue to drink from what the world has to offer, but remember, we'll continue to thirst again and again.

But whoever drinks of the water that I shall give him will never thirst. But the water that I shall give him will become in him a fountain of water springing up into everlasting life. – John 4:14

DAY 22
MY HEART IS GOD'S HOME

One of the most amazing things about giving our lives to God, is that we get to give Him access to the very core of our hearts, and this is where He dwells and makes His home. We know the heart as one of the vital organs in our body, and that it pumps blood to all of our other organs. So when I began to read about the heart in the bible, I had a lot of questions. I mean, of course God doesn't physically take your human heart out and replace it with a new one, and I knew that. I just didn't fully understand that we also have a spiritual heart, and that it is just as vital and central to our spiritual being as the physical heart is to our physical being.

Next, I read that the heart is deceitful. WHAT? If my heart is deceitful, then why would God choose to live there of all places? My heart is the only department that is classified as deceitful and yet God not only wants it, but He wants to live there? Oh, did I have questions! After much researching, I came to an understanding that the heart is deceitful because it's so easily influenced by people, and the things we entertain ourselves with. As we read the scriptures, we see that most of the issues of life are matters of the heart and how we perceive things. No wonder why Solomon tells us to guard it describes the heart as the wellsprings of life (Proverbs 4:23). This is literally where you draw from, and this is where your motives and intentions lie. This is why we have to guard our hearts because what we allow in it may become toxic, which in return affects everything we do.

I think the biggest challenge is figuring out what we need to look out for and how to go about guarding ourselves.

Below are some guidelines to put "guarding your heart" into more practical terms, and will also help to illustrate the different departments that make up the spiritual heart and the rooms that we're to give Him access to. Here is an excerpt from Joyce Meyer's "Letting God into every room of your heart"- which really helped me put things into a more clear perspective:

*'**The Study or the Library:** Our mind. What kind of things do you think about? The more you think of something, the more it becomes a part of you. In fact, your thoughts set the course for your life. God knows what we're thinking, so let's focus on things that He wants us to think-things that are noble, pure, trustworthy, admirable...(see Philippians 4:8). And remember, you can choose what you think about. So when the devil tries to interject thoughts in your mind, you don't have to just take them.*

***Dining Room:** Our Desires. We need to come to the point where we can say "God, I only want what You want, and if I'm asking for something You don't want me to have, then don't give it to me." Our desires can cause the biggest problems in our life-especially when someone else gets something we want. But God wants us to be happy for others when they are blessed and trust that He'll do what is best for us at the right time.*

***The Living or Family Room:** Your Friends. Who are your friends? What do you talk about when you're with your friends? I'm talking here about the people you spend your time with and those you open your heart to. Does your conversation put a smile on God's face...or does it grieve Him? Get together with people who love the Word of God and be creative with how you help others. Because there's one thing for sure: when you get your mind off yourself and focus on blessing someone else, you'll get happier than you've ever been!*

***The Workroom:** Your Legacy. Are you bearing good fruit...or are you just taking up space? I encourage you to work with excellence and integrity. When you choose not to gossip at work, waste company time or participate in things that wouldn't please Him, then you honor God. And when you* honor God, then He will honor you. *Remember: We need to do what's right because it's right, even when no one's looking...because God is always with us.*

Recreation Room: *Your Entertainment. Do you let God decide what movies you watch, the music you listen to or the things you read? There is nothing wrong with having a good time, but our choices also need to honor Him. Likewise, we have to be careful about how much time we devote to entertainment. When it takes a stronger priority in our life than it should, there's a problem. It's not that you can't have any fun; you just need to choose what is best for you and is pleasing to God.*

The Hall, Closet, Attic, Garage or Basement: *Hidden Things. This is where we hide all those things we don't think we'll use again, but we hold on to them just in case...things like self-pity or unforgiveness. God dealt strongly with me about self-pity. But even after I officially gave it up, I put it somewhere in that back closet of my life just in case I wanted to have just one more pity party. How about getting rid of everything that's not pleasing to God?*

These are some of the compartments that make up our spiritual heart. Take time to truly examine them, making room for the King of all Kings to live there.

The heart is more deceitful than all else, and is desperately wicked; who can understand it? I, The Lord, search the heart, I test the mind, even to give each man according to his ways, according to the results of His deeds. – Jeremiah 17:9-10

DAY 23
THE STORMS OF LIFE

When we hear about an imminent storm, or when we are amidst one; our first impulse is to run for cover, bolt our entryways, and find sufficient protection. You *rarely* hear of anyone deliberately going out into the storm or even really embracing it.

When it comes to rain, wind, and thunder - while the majority of the other birds take off and run for cover, the eagle flies specifically to it. There is something in the storm that the eagle sees and is built to face that the other birds are not. The eagle uses the turbulence from a storm to push it higher into the sky, they utilize the bad weather as an entryway for higher heights; heights that they couldn't reach in good weather. When they achieve that new height, it allows them to coast and rest their wings.

We can also look at life's turbulence from an eagle's perspective. Jesus said in John 16:33 that we would have many troubles in this life; but He also left us with the tools to rise above them. When troubles and hardship ascend, instead of running for cover, we can utilize these circumstances as an opportunity to achieve higher statures. Instead, we can transform what might seem like a loss, into gains by standing firm on the word of God.

At times, in order to fortify our strength, faith, or achieve new heights in Christ, we need to experience hardships. These rough times strengthen our fellowship with God and are also a declaration to our own selves of how much God is on our side.

Blessed is the man who remains steadfast under trial, for when he has stood the test he will receive the crown of life, which God has promised to those who love him. James 1:12

DAY 24
FAITH > FEAR

Satan will always try to find a way to cripple every godly endeavor in your life with fear - the fear of failure, the fear of lacking, the fear of loneliness, or the fear of rejection. These are all common tools that he will use to block you from who God's called you to be, or what you're called to do.

It's crucial that we understand what fear is, and how it can keep us outside of the will and plan of God if we allow it to stick around.

In 1 Timothy 1:7, we are reminded that God did not give us a spirit of fear, but of power, love, and a sound mind.

The truth is, while we do not voluntarily choose to feel fear, it's an emotion that rises up within every so often. We may become fearful when starting a new job, starting a life with a spouse, starting a business, or moving out on our own. In Psalm 56:3 – David wrote "when I am afraid, I will put my trust in you". God wants us to turn to Him in moments that we are afraid so that He can replace these thoughts with courage.

When you give your life to Jesus Christ, you become brand new creature. This means, whatever Jesus says about you, is what you are. God wants us to step out in spite of fear and not bow down to it. Accept this truth in your heart that God is with you. He has no intention of failing you. Trust the One Who knitted you together and is your beginning and your end.

Have I not commanded you? Be strong and courageous. Do not be afraid; do not be discouraged, for the LORD your God will be with you wherever you go. – Joshua 1:9

DAY 25
AN INVITATION TO ABUNDANT LIFE

I get extremely excited when I receive wedding invitations in my mailbox. There's something about weddings that cause me to become overly excited. Within days, I'm keeping an eye out for a new dress and thinking about what I'm going to do with my hair. Most of us can agree that it's an honor knowing that someone thought of you to celebrate such a milestone in their life and a privilege that you have made it on the guest list.

I know that we're used to traditional invites that come with a return address folded in a pretty envelope, tied with a ribbon, instructions for gift registries, and RSVP deadlines. But did you know that there is also an invitation from our Heavenly Father that works far beyond our thoughts and understanding? He has extended an invitation to abundant life, and I don't know what could be better than an invite to an overflow of joy, peace, wealth, patience, wisdom, virtue, and strength.

There is perfect peace in knowing that while Satan comes to steal, kill, and destroy; Jesus came so that we may have life, and have it more abundantly – *John 10:10*. I've lived on both ends of the spectrum. I lived a life outside of Christ, and now, I live a life in Christ. I can say with all my heart that life in Christ is by far the best life, and there's nothing this world can offer me to change that.

Jesus is asking us to respond to this invitation by doing one simple thing....just come. Those who are thirsty, come! Those who have no money, come! Those who are sick, come! For anyone who is burdened, come! There is only one way to respond to this invitation and we don't have to spend our money on new dresses, new shoes, or on hundreds of dollars on gifts. God is saying, "just come".

Everyone who thirsts, come to the waters; And you who have no money, come, buy and eat. Yes, come, buy wine and milk without money and without price. Why do you spend money for *what is* not bread, and your wages for *what* does not satisfy? Listen carefully to Me, and eat *what is* good, and let your soul delight itself in abundance. - Isaiah 55: 1-2

TO SEEK AND TO SAVE

If being guilty by association was an actual offense, I'm certain Jesus would have been convicted and charged in His days here on earth. He had a radical position associating Himself with those who were lost by sharing the truth of the gospel through friendship and love.

I remember when I had a beautiful pair of Swarovski earrings, and ended up losing one of them in a hotel room with a few friends from my church. I practically ripped the room to pieces looking for them. They were valuable to me and I went through a huge deal of effort to find the lost one. The same would be true if you owned an animal and lost it, you would go to great lengths to find your pet by walking or driving through neighborhoods, putting up pictures, and maybe even offering a ransom until it was found.

Luke 19:1-10 explains the story of Zacchaeus, a very wealthy, scheming, and greedy tax collector who cheated people out of money. Zacchaeus was in a town called Jericho and hears of Jesus coming. While Jesus was walking through the crowds, Zacchaeus climbs a sycamore tree to get a better look of Jesus. As Jesus is passing by, He calls for Zacchaeus and says *"come down! I must be a guest in your home today."* Zacchaeus comes down, takes Jesus to his home and the crowd was livid! They knew who Zacchaeus was - a notorious sinner, and yet Jesus wanted to be a guest in his home?

After one encounter with Jesus, Zacchaeus offers to give half of his wealth to the poor, and give back four times the amount that he stole from people. Jesus obviously didn't condone his behavior, but *Luke 10:10* says that *"the Son of Man came to seek and save who are lost.*" This is the heart of Jesus and the continual theme of Luke's gospel. Jesus went everywhere seeking that one lost sheep. It amazes me that Jesus is willing to leave ninety-nine of the sheep by his side just to find the one who is lost. He values every single one of us in this same manner and went the extra mile by coming here on earth to seek and to save us.

We were all once lost and rightly deserved God's judgement until Jesus came. If we are to follow His example of seeking lost sheep, we must show the same effort He did, as if it were one of our valuables – or in my case, my crystal earrings.

Through Luke's gospel, we have been challenged to consider our hearts toward the lost. Are we willing to go the extra mile to share the love of Jesus and bring love, fellowship, and truth to the life of someone else as He did?

If a man has a hundred sheep and one of them gets lost, what will he do? Won't he leave the ninety-nine others in the wilderness and go to search for the one that is lost until he finds it? And when he has found it, he will joyfully carry it home on his shoulders. When he arrives, he will call together his friends and neighbors saying, "Rejoice with me because I have found my lost sheep." In the same way there is more joy in heaven over one lost sinner who repents and returns to God, that over ninety-nine others who are righteous and haven't strayed away. – Luke 15:3-7

DAY 27
UNDEFEATED

God assures us in *Jeremiah 29:11* that He knows plans He has for us, and those plans incorporate peace, a future, and hope. We may start to ask ourselves how this makes sense with all that is going on in the world right now? How could there be peace when there are wars? How can I look towards the future, but every other year there are threats of global warming and the world coming to an end? How does this bode well when for the greater part of our lives it's been a fight, and feels like we've been built up just to be let down?

It seems as though the state of defeat is working overtime in the lives of humanity right now, and we might ask ourselves if God is who He says He is; why am I still in this wreckage? Why do I feel like I am walking around as a defeated being? You may be experiencing restless nights or waking up and instantly being assaulted with the stresses of life. You may have read self-help books and the Bible, and yet the cycle of the state of defeat prevails. We know that feeling defeated contradicts the life that Christ intends for us to live. So knowing that, why does the road ahead still look bleak?

When we understand everything Jesus came on this earth to accomplish, we understand that defeat has no place in our lives. This doesn't guarantee that trials won't arise, but through those trials, we can still remain victors.

When Jesus was here on earth, those who crucified Him presumably giggled and rejoiced once He was put in His tomb - believing that He was now defeated. Keep in mind, today that tomb is empty. Regardless of what Jesus had to endure, He remained consistent with His identity amid the darkest hours of His life, and remained steadfast and confident in the triumph to come. So, take rest in knowing that you are not defeated, and you're already victors because that's His very plan for you!

For I know the thoughts that I think toward you, says the LORD, thoughts of peace and not of evil, to give you a future and a hope. – Jeremiah 29:11

DAY 28
PINKY PROMISE

As little kids and even in our teenage or adolescent lives, one of the many things that we do to bind or solidify a friendship is the exchange of a promise one to another. The oath may vary from the promise to always be friends, or the promise never to share secrets that have been exchanged.

Unfortunately, because of our fragile and unstable human nature, we've had promises towards us broken, or have sometimes been the one to break a promise. So when we hear or read of the promises of God, in our human nature, we often doubt what He is saying or respond with an "I'll believe it when I see it" kind of attitude.

So what makes the promises of God so special when the earth is filled with broken promises? To understand how valuable God's promises are, we first have to understand His nature. The bible says that *"God is not like man, that He should lie" (Number 23:19)*. That means whatever comes out of His mouth is the truth, and He is more than capable of fulfilling the promises that He's made.

There is no way to measure the greatness of God. This is one of the reasons He gives us circumstances in life that are beyond our abilities to solve, so that we can experience a fraction of what He's capable of. When He makes a promise, He intends on keeping it. It's a matter of faith, patience, and being grateful for the promises already fulfilled. If you're facing what seems like an impossible situation right now, be encouraged by standing on the very promise of God. When God gives us assurance; He has the power to follow through.

Having an attitude of gratitude and excitement will encourage God to move on your behalf. God is not impressed by doubt and bad attitudes. He wants us to get excited because He has spoken and wants us to believe Him.

In Philippians 4:7 – He promised a peace that surpasses all understanding.
In Romans 6:23 – He promised eternal life through His son Jesus.
In Jeremiah 29:11 – He promised a future and hope.
In Mathew 11:28-29 – He promised us rest.
In Philippians 4:19 – He promised to supply all of our needs according to His riches in glory.

These are just a few of the promises given to us. How encouraging is it to know that God would commit Himself to do anything else according to His will for us? His ways are not our ways and His thoughts are far beyond us, yet He responds to our deepest fears and doubts by giving us hope through His promises. Today we can choose to rest in the unfailing and unshakable Word of God, and believe that we will see His goodness towards us right here in the land of the living.

By his divine power, God has given us everything we need for living a godly life. We have received all of this by coming to know Him, the one who called us to Himself by means of His marvelous glory and excellence. And because of His glory and excellence, He has given us great and precious promises. These are the promises that enable you to share His divine nature and escape the world's corruption caused by human desires.- 2 Peter 1:3-4

DAY 29
BEAUTY IS FLEETING

It's easy to base our worth and value on all of the wrong things in a generation where cosmetics and superficial values have completely taken over. It's no surprise that some women are finding it almost impossible to measure up to the world's standard of what beauty is. We are going to extreme lengths to look a certain way or possess a certain image and I strongly believe that women are more insecure with their image today than they have ever been.

I don't say this to condemn cosmetics, fashion, or the need to be well-groomed. Rather, I want to point our attention to the fact that women are now finding it impossible to find true beauty outside of what the media portrays.

When God began to restructure my understanding of feminine beauty, I realized how far off I was for a large chunk of my life. It took a while for me to understand the balance in presenting myself well while not placing my worth on my outer image. It's important that we understand God has no problem with us putting ourselves together and looking presentable (after all, we are daughters of a King). But He doesn't want us obsessing over superficial standards of beauty.

God wants to give us a completely different view of what it means to be beautiful. Proverbs 31:30 says that "favor is deceitful and beauty is vain, but a woman who fears The Lord, she shall be praised". Outer beauty eventually deteriorates, and our looks will change. We won't always have smooth skin, and let's face it, gravity eventually takes over. But what won't change is our love for God and the inward attributes that never fade.

If we spend more time with The One who made us in His image, it will invite a true sense of beauty within us. You can ask God to remove false confidence, and anything or anyone that makes you believe or feel you are not beautiful enough. With or without the enhancers, you are beautiful, just the way God designed you, from the number of hairs on your head to the different colors of your skin, you are beautiful!

Today, you can start to focus on your inner beauty - it starts by exchanging all that you are for all that God is. He will give you a supernatural glow that cannot be bought over the counter. He wants to give you a beauty that will make you shine from the inside out. Exodus 34:29 tells us that when Moses spent 40 days and 40 nights with God, His face started shining. There is no contour kit or highlighters that can give you that kind of glow outside of spending time in the presence of the King of Kings.

Your beauty should not come from outward adornments, such as elaborate hairstyles and the wearing of gold jewelry or fine clothes. Rather, it should be that of your inner self, the unfading beauty of a gentle and quiet spirit, which is of great worth in God's sight. - 1 Peter 3:3-4

DAY 30
I'M HERE ON PURPOSE!

If you were asked to complete this one sentence….. "My purpose in life is to_____" what would you have filled in the blank with? Some of us may have quickly said "to give God glory" or to "help people/spread the gospel". This, of course, is not a wrong response. In fact, God wants us to do these things; but if we're truly coming from an honest place, that may not be our sincere answer.

One of the most frequent questions you will hear on this planet is "why am I here?" We're all told that we have a purpose in life and that we were born for a reason. One day, I started to reflect on what that reason was, and why I was born. I remember throughout this time, I was attending the youth service at my church, and my Youth Pastor at the time said this one phrase that has stuck with me over the last 5 years: "Your purpose is not a destination, but a journey". If nothing else changed my view of what purpose meant - that surely did. I had to stop looking at my purpose as this place I would one day "arrive" to, and start looking at it as a day-to-day journey. So the question still remained – what is my purpose? Or better yet, how can I live out my purpose on a daily basis?

A lot of self-help books may tell you that the answer in finding your purposes lies "within you," and we may even go as far as taking personality tests to answer our deepest question, "why am I here?" The truth is, self-help books may indeed help, but they do not provide the ultimate answer. Our purpose is something only God can reveal to us, essentially because it's not "our purpose" but it is His purpose for us. Most of us may end up missing the mark because of our complex search for direction, from sources outside of the One who created us.

The biggest lie that you will ever hear in your life is that "you have no purpose". You may not have been born in ideal circumstances, but even if your parents didn't plan you, God did. God had you on His mind before you were even formed in the womb. *Psalm 139:16* says "*You saw me before I was born. Every day of my life was recorded in Your book. Every moment was laid out before a single day had passed.*"

Regardless of what circumstances you were born under, God knew you before you were born and had every single day of your life recorded. God's purpose for your life overrides any human error made by your parents or those around you. We may have had illegitimate circumstances, but there is no such thing as an illegitimate child.

The Bible reminds us in multiple ways that we were created on purpose and for a reason:

You were created to have a relationship with God
Leviticus 26:11-12 - I will live among you, and I will not despise you. I will walk among you; and I will be your God, and you will be My people.

You were created to do Gods work
Ephesians 2:10 - For we are Gods workmanship, created in Christ Jesus to do good works, which God prepared in advance for us to do.

You were created to bring God glory
Isaiah 43:6-7 – Bring my sons and daughters back to Israel from the distant corners of the earth. Bring all who claim me as their God, for I have made them for My glory, it was I who created them.

You were created to use the gifts God gave you
1 Peter 4:10 – As each has received a gift, use it to serve one another, as good stewards of God's varied grace.

We can stop entertaining the lies that Satan whispers in our ears: the lie that you were a mistake, the lie that you have no talents, the lie that you're not good enough, the lie that your situation is too horrible for God to use you, the lie that you are too old, and the lie that you are too young.

God's plan is for the present. Your life has profound meaning, and you were made for a reason.

In him we have obtained an inheritance, having been predestined according to the purpose of him who works all things according to the counsel of his will. – Ephesians 1:11

References:

Joyce Meyer – Letting God into every room of your heart
www.crossmap.com

www.psycologytoday.com

www.openbible.info

The Holy Bible, KJV & NLT version

Printed in Great Britain
by Amazon